THE FOUNDER

THE LIFE OF THOMAS WRIOTHESLEY, THE FIRST EARL OF SOUTHAMPTON

BRYAN DUNLEAVY

THE FOUNDER

THE LIFE OF THOMAS WRIOTHESLEY, THE FIRST EARL OF SOUTHAMPTON

BRYAN DUNLEAVY

Published by the Titchfield History Society 2023

ISBN 978-1-915166-05-0

www.titchfieldhistory.co.uk

A catalogue description of this book is available from the British Library

FIRST YEARS

The story of Thomas Wriothesley, while not exactly a rags to riches tale, is nevertheless a remarkable one. He was born into a middle ranking family but at his death at the age of 45 was one of the richest men in the country.

His father was William Writh, Windsor Herald, a younger son of John Writh, (sometimes referred to as Sir John Writh) who had been Garter King at Arms throughout the reign of Henry VII. He therefore inhabited the court work with duties that encompassed some diplomatic functions as well as the important medieval administration of heraldry. We can assume that he was well paid for his services. John Writh's eldest son took over the role of Garter from his father. The family were well-established in this line of work.

The Writh family originated in Wiltshire and may have established themselves in London as grocers - a prosperous trade. Leading merchant families frequently put their sons forward as suitable candidates for court position. One might recall Geoffrey Chaucer in the 14th century who, as the son of a prosperous merchant, easily moved into the diplomatic role that became his career.

The elder brother of William laid claim to the more important sounding name of Wriothesley. He was part of a rising middle class in the early 16th century who tried, where they could, to embellish the status of their families. It was said, for example, that the Wriths on one side of the family could claim descent from an illegitimate child of Henry I. Since that energetic king fathered at least twenty bastard children, the claim is not implausible. He made the case that Wriothesley was the original family name and the claim was not challenged and he persuaded his younger brother to take up the name. Thus William's eldest son Thomas was baptised Thomas Wriothesley.

Thomas was born on 21 December 1505 in London. His mother was Jane Drayton. Little is known about her family, although it is assumed that her father was a London merchant. There was a younger brother, Edward, and two sisters. He was only 8 years old when his father died, probably at the age of 40, but this does not seem to have materially impacted on the family. Thomas was able to attend William Lily's school at St Pauls and later went to Trinity Hall, Cambridge. Aside from his education he was able to make contacts with people who also became influential figures in Tudor Government. He was at school with Anthony Denney, Edward North, William Paget, each of whom went on to distinguished careers in government and the writer John Leland. At Trinity he met Stephen Gardiner, who became a friend and colleague and the powerful Bishop of

Winchester.

IN THE OFFICE OF CARDINAL WOLSEY

At the age of 19, in 1524, Wriothesley was recorded as a clerk in the office of Cardinal Wolsey, the most powerful figure in the land, next to the king. It was a prime posting and the Cardinal, always on the lookout for bright young men, must have been impressed Wriothesley's gifts. His young protégé quickly made his mark and in 1525 he was entrusted with managing the complex arrangements that led to the foundation of the college now know as Christ's Church College at Oxford. This was a complex exercise on land acquisition and management. Funds were raised through the dissolution of several small monasteries, a long time before the general dissolution of the 1530s. The site for the new college was St Frideswide's monastery at Oxford, a short distance from Carfax. The monks had to be relocated and the buildings demolished to make space for the new buildings.

These arrangements could not be simple. The inmates of the monastery could not be cast out on the streets to fend for themselves and the transaction involved finding new placements or by awarding pensions. This was a significant task for the young man and we can assume that he acquitted himself well because the work on the new college proceeded as intended. In addition, several small priories across the country were dissolved to fund this new foundation.

Once his career was established he felt secure enough to get married

Cardinal Wolsey and Thomas Cromwell

and start a family. He married Jane Cheney, a daughter of Sir William Cheney from the Chalfont area of Buckinghamshire. As to when they married we can only guess. Some say before 1533 but it could have been earlier. His daughter Elizabeth married in 1545 to Thomas Radcliffe, later Earl of Sussex. The marriage had been arranged in 1543 so the actual date two years later might suggest that they waited until at least she was 14, or possibly 16. If it was 14, her birth would be 1531, offering us a potential wedding year of 1530 between Thomas Wriothesley and Jane Cheyney. Since Wriothesley was appointed Clerk of the Signet in 1530, this date may be about right.

As to their children some names can be pieced together from various sources. There was a William, most likely the first born son named after his two grandfathers and Anthony. Both died as either infants or small children and we only know of their existence through a notebook left by the Countess. William died in August 1537 at about the age of two and Anthony died in 1542. The third son, Henry, was born quite late, in 1546, and lived to become the second earl and inherited his father's estates upon his majority.

Wriothesley's position as one of the Clerks of the Signet moved him to a senior position at the heart of government, and he continued to advance during this decade. By 1530 the Cardinal's power was waning due to his inability to resolve the matter of the king's divorce. Such high matters of state were above Wriothesley's level of importance at the time, but he could have lost office when the great Cardinal fell from grace in 1530. It may have been coincidental or planned, but in 1530 Thomas Wriothesley attached himself to the office of Thomas Cromwell. Cromwell had been occupied with freelance legal work for government but in January 1530 he sought, and was granted, a position in the king's service. Thus began the most fruitful association of Thomas Wriothesley's career.

CROMWELL'S RIGHT HAND MAN

After the fall of Wolsey Cromwell gradually became the king's chief councillor. He was a clever man and for his time a very modern thinker. He has been credited with the idea that the king could be the head of the church, although it is possible that the first thought came from the junior Thomas Wriothesley. There was a letter written by Wriothesley in 1532 that developed the argument that a judge was only able to bring into effect judgements within his own jurisdiction, and therefore Henry, in this case, could not be compelled to obey judgements from Rome since England was not subject to Roman law. Henry married Anne Boleyn in January 1533 and in May Archbishop Cranmer pronounced the divorce from Catherine.

To further legalise matters Henry assumed the title of Supreme Head of the Church in England in June 1534. He was no longer beholden to the Pope.

Henry appointed Cromwell as his principal secretary in April 1534 to replace Stephen Gardiner, bishop of Winchester. The powerful prelate was always a difficult man, and Henry had had enough. By this time Cromwell was the obvious alternative to replace him. Wriothesley was promoted to become one of Henry's secretaries, so the two men now worked together on a daily basis.

Wriothesley was a useful man. He was highly intelligent and hard working and he had the necessary skills to get things done. During this period he managed the office and saw to the day to day transactions while Cromwell looked after higher matters of state. And after the Act of Supremacy, one of the highest matters of state was religious reform. These were momentous years and the radical reform of religious houses created the conditions for a more vibrant economy. Wriothesley may not have foreseen the long term impact of his efforts, but he was intimately involved in the implementation of this policy.

Thomas Cromwell is usually seen as the architect and prime mover in the General Dissolution of the 1530s, and to some extent there is truth in that. But his initial instinct was to reform houses rather than close them down. Commissioners were sent out in 1535 to assess and value all religious houses, and they compiled what is known as the *Valor Ecclesiasticus*. However the report exposed corruption in several religious houses and this led to a determination to effect comprehensive reform. An Act of Suppression received royal assent on 14 April 1536. Houses with an income of under £200 a year were to be suppressed. The work proceeded immediately. For the most part the process was benign. Legal form was observed and the monks were suitably compensated with alternative livings, transfer to larger houses, or granted pensions. Some of the higher placed individuals did very well out of it.

Wriothesley was nothing if not hard headed when it came to effecting this policy. He personally supervised the confiscation of the treasures of the shrine of St Thomas Becket at Canterbury and at St Swithun's at Winchester. The former was probably the most politically sensitive and probably needed a senior figure, such as Wriothesley had now become, to ensure that Crown wishes were put into effect. At Winchester the shrine to St Swithun was dismantled in the middle of the night to avoid any possible public outcry. He also made sure that various local officials were present to verify the act. Wriothesley wrote to Cromwell to assure him that the shrines at both places had been destroyed. He then proceeded to the abbeys of St Mary's and Hyde in Winchester "to sweep away all the bones that be called relics" Similar action was taken at Chichester in December 1538 when the bones of St Richard, a former bishop, were disposed of. There is no doubt that once given a task he performed it zealously and to perfection.

That is one side of Wriothesley, but in the same period we see other aspects. He is clearly seen as an influential figure in Cromwell's office and he received letters from many who looked to him to help them acquire new property. The Earl of Northumberland wrote to him to ask him to arrange a meeting with Cromwell. The Earl of Rutland also wrote a letter expressing his interest in Croxton Abbey. In December 1536 Sir John Tregonwell wrote to ask for assistance in obtaining the nunnery of St Giles in Hertfordshire. John Husee wrote to Lord Lisle in February 1537 advising his patron to "make a friend of him; the man standeth in a place where he may please or displease."[1] Hussee (and Lord Lisle) were to be disappointed because 18 months later he was writing that Wriothesley's promises were about as dependable as holy water - in other words worthless.

In the course of this work Wriothesley was able to make a great deal of money - a small fortune in fact. As a king's official he was entitled to receive a payment or gift for access. We would regard this as corruption today but for these men it was a natural source of income. Tax gatherers were expected to keep back a percentage of what they collected for their "trouble" and, in the same manner, the law was administered on the basis of payments to the judge. Wriothesley was in a position to benefit. Durham Cathedral for example gave Wriothesley a pension, as well as similar amounts to Cromwell and Seymour, in the hope that the dissolution would bypass their cathedral.

The downfall of Thomas Cromwell in 1540 was very swift, and quite arbitrary.

On New Years Day 1540, Henry left Greenwich to meet his bride to be, Anne of Cleves, when she arrived in England. Nothing seemed untoward at the time but when Cromwell asked the king how he found his prospective wife, he was astonished at the response. "She is nothing so fair as she has been reported."[2] Henry certainly discussed with his councillors ways of avoiding the marriage but reluctantly went ahead with it anyway. From later reports it is understood that he made no serious attempt at consummating the marriage.

For a time the issue died and everyone returned to normal business.

1 Gibbons, Geoffrey. *The Political Career of Thomas Wriothesley, First Earl of Southampton, 1505-1550*. (University of Warwick, 1999). p 43

2 Schofield, John. *The Rise and Fall of Thomas Cromwell: Henry VIII's Most Faithful Servant*. (Stroud: The History Press, 2011) p 361

Cromwell was elevated to the earldom of Essex on 18 April, which surely would not have happened if he had been out of favour with the king. What really disrupted the equilibrium was that the youthful Catherine Howard was deliberately paraded before the king. The Duke of Norfolk and others had seen their opportunity. If (and they did succeed) they could tempt the king to take the bait and divorce Anne, then the marriage to Catherine would restore the Howards to the centre of power. This would also enable them to proceed against Cromwell and the reformers and return the church to the old faith .Cromwell was acting in the best interests of the state and in fashioning this marriage he was certainly doing something which would strengthen Englands hand in European alliances. Henry was by now becoming increasingly autocratic and identified his personal wishes with statecraft. He did not find Anne attractive, but married her anyway and felt resentful that he had been engineered into this marriage. He blamed Cromwell and Cromwell's enemies, Norfolk and Gardiner, were quick to take the opportunity to blacken Cromwell's name.

Cromwell was arrested on June 10th in the Council chamber. Norfolk led the party but Cromwell's former associates, FitzWilliam, Paget and Wriothesley were also involved in the reduction of their former master. Paget and Wriothesley were assigned to interrogate Cromwell, which they did without showing any deference to their former patron.

The swiftness in Wriothesley's action in turning his personal craft into the prevailing wind shows us a man who was able to act without sentimentality. He was not the only one to turn on Cromwell but he was assiduous in prosecuting the demands of the king. Much of the deposition prepared by Wriothesley for Cromwell's trial was, to put no fine point on it, unhelpful to Cromwell and to our eyes today was designed to prove his treason. He also ignored Thomas Cromwell's requests to explain himself to the king and to all intents abandoned the drowning man.

The line to be taken was that Henry was misled into the marriage with Anne of Cleves and it was all Cromwell's doing. The fact that ambassadors on the spot sent glowing reports about Anne's character and personality and that Cromwell had kept Henry informed every step along the way were all ignored in favour of this new interpretation. It has to be said that Wriothesley himself had been very much involved in the policy that led to the marriage and was clearly anxious to distance himself from it. Wriothesley's hand is all over these documents. He was also sent, along with Earl Suffolk and Fitzwilliam, to meet with the queen herself and persuade her to agree to the divorce. Anne showed herself to be politically astute. In return for a house in Lewes, a household staff and an annual income of £4000 she agreed to the divorce and to adopt a quiet life out of sight and out of mind. She died in 1557.

A Man of Property

Two years before this, Thomas Wriothesley had used his privileged position and his accumulated wealth to create a remarkable property portfolio. By the mid-1530s Sir Thomas Wriothesley had been able to fill chests with coins. He had been able to live well in London, but his income far exceeded his outgoings and he was in a position to embark on a major campaign of land acquisition. The moment was right. The dissolution of the monasteries flooded the market with new properties. Moreover, he was in a prime position to take his pick of what was on offer. The reason why he focussed his attention on Hampshire is unknown. He came from a Wiltshire family and he had spent all his life in London. Nevertheless, he picked out prime properties in Hampshire and in the process became one of the largest landowners in the County. He was able to purchase the monasteries of Titchfield, Hyde in Winchester, Beaulieu in the New Forest and Quarr on the Isle of Wight. Each came with substantial landholdings.

At the end of 1537 he acquired the abbey of Titchfield, together with its associated manors. He almost immediately set about creating his country seat at Titchfield and the new house was to remain of some importance until it was pulled down in the 18th century. The abbey was founded in 1222 with the endowment of the manor of Titchfield and some neighboring manors. Further grants of land enlarged the abbey's holdings so that by the time of the dissolution most of the land between Stokes Bay and the River Hamble, together with manors at Porchester and Cosham and along the New Forest side of Southampton Water, were under the sway of the abbey. Further up the Meon Valley, parts of Wickham, Soberton, Corhampton and West Meon were annexed to the abbey, with the later addition of a manor in Berkshire. It had become quite a wealthy abbey, and the canons could even afford to maintain a large library. When Sir Thomas Wriothesley acquired the abbey the true wealth lay in the extensive lands.

There is no record of what Wriothesley paid for this. Unlike Beaulieu, where a sum was paid to the Crown, there is no record for Titchfield. Thus we can only speculate. The best guess, given that much was arranged in advance, is that Wriothesley himself took responsibility for all of the costs of acquisition. He took on the pensions for the canons, paid off the debts and any other expenses associated with the takeover. £50 a year covered the pensions, which, allowing for an outside average of 20 years, amounted to £1000. There was a debt of £200 and there may have been other costs, such as presents for the commissioners and others who helped with the takeover. The total may have approached £1400. By any measure this was this was

Place House as it appeared in 1780

Part of the ruins of Beaulieu Abbey.

the deal of the century. The outlay would be recovered in five to six years income from this huge estate - 15,000 acres.

Wriothesley lost little time in putting his plans into effect. Most of the old monastery buildings were dismantled. Stone and marble were sold off as were the abbey bells. The work of building the new palace or place could now begin. Quality stone was imported from Caen for the facing.

The earliest eye witness to this new building was the antiquary John Leland who was able to report:

> Mr Wriothesley hath builded a right stately house embatelid, and having a goodely Gate and a conducte castelid in the Midle of the Court of it, yn the very same Place wher the late Monasterie of Premostrantences stoode caullyd Tichefelde.[3]

The nave of the old abbey church was kept as the core of the new house, and it appears that the cloisters were also retained as a quadrangle to the north of the house. The Wriothesley additions were the gate house turrets in the centre and two residential wings on either side. They also added a new building on the west side of the cloisters, probably as a kitchen.[4]

Quarr Abbey and Hyde Abbey were both demolished and the salvaged building materials sold off. The real wealth, in any case, was in the land, and Hyde Abbey had owned several lucrative manors in central Hampshire. Beaulieu Abbey was put 'beyond use' as was required by the government, but little else was done with it at this stage.

His other significant purchase in this period was the Bloomsbury manor on the outskirts of London. It had belonged to the Carthusian monks of

The gatehouse of Place House as it appears today.

3 Chandler, John. *John Leland's Itinerary.* (Stroud: The History Press, 2011). iii, 111.
4 See *The Making of Place House:* The Titchfield Papers, no 7, (Titchfield History Society, 2021). ISBN: 9780993421388

London's Charterhouse and in 1547 it was, as one of Henry VIII's last acts, granted to Baron Titchfield. In centuries to come it was to prove to be the most valuable asset of the Wriothesley family.

The 1540s marked Wriothesley's years of greatest power and prosperity. They often showed him at his best as an efficient administrator of the Crown's affairs, but his efforts to restrain the trend towards Protestantism often brought out the worst aspects of his personality.

AT THE HEART OF GOVERNMENT

Thomas Wriothesley was officially appointed secretary to the Privy Council in April 1540 and he was knighted at the same time. He held the position jointly with Ralph Sadler and it appears that there was more than enough work to divide between them without any competition between them. However it appears that Wriothesley had been acting in this role for two years prior to this date. Henry identifies Wriothesley as one of his secretaries in September 1538[5] and two letters written by John Godsalve to "his right worshipful cousin Mr Wriothesley, one of the kinge highnes secretaryes"[6]

He was knighted in 1540 and on 1 January 1544 created Baron Wriothesley of Titchfield, a title he held until the death of the king.

Soon after, on April 21st 1544 Sir Thomas Audley, ill and near death, resigned as Lord Chancellor. He was a competent lawyer and perhaps closer to the point in the perilous world of Henrician court politics was not politically ambitious. He was therefore able to occupy the position he took upon the execution of Sir Thomas More in 1531 and hold it. The real political power in those years lay with Thomas Cromwell who as Principal Secretary and Lord Privy Seal was the real heir to Cardinal Wolsey.

The post of Lord Chancellor had for many years been filled by senior churchmen. In Tudor times, the role had been taken by men with legal training, such as Sir Thomas More and Sir Thomas Audley. As far as we know, Thomas Wriothesley had no training in legal matters, although he may well have picked up sufficient knowledge through his years at court. In this respect he was an odd choice; however, he was sufficiently trusted by Henry and sufficiently proven as a court official to be given the role.

Wriothesley's greatest ability was in financial management and his instincts were to concentrate on the financial and administrative aspects of the Chancellorship rather than the legal, however, these legal commitments were not negligible. The two previous incumbents had, over 15 years, made

---

5 Letters and Papers xiii (2) 418.
6 PRO SP 1/150 fo 125, SP 7/1 (LP xiv (1), 757)

the Chancery court pre-eminent in dealing with land disputes. The Lord Chancellor was also president of the Court of the Star Chamber.

Thomas Wriothesley had some legal training but had worked more as an administrator than a lawyer;

The politics of the 1540s, in the last years of Henry VIII, now an old king, had changed from the 1530s. Whereas the evangelicals and the conservatives could find common cause in the need to reform the old medieval church, the conservative no longer wished to go as far as the protestant reformers wanted

The drive against heretics gathered pace in 1540. Cromwell, a reformer and Lutheran sympathies, had been seen off by his enemies. Once he had been beheaded on 28 July 1540, the conservative, including Wriothesley, embarked on a campaign against heretics. There were several high profile executions.

Even Archbishop Cranmer became a target. Gardiner encouraged seven conservative canons of Canterbury Cathedral to bring forward complaints that Cranmer was encouraging heretical sermons within his diocese. These written accusations were delivered to Henry, who, because he liked Cranmer, appointed him to head a commission of inquiry into the accusations. To no surprise the accusations came to nothing.

Cranmer was once more a target in 1545 when the conservative thought they had detected heresies in primer the archbishop had published that summer. Henry was told and agreed to Cranmer's arrest at the Privy Council meeting the following day. Henry once more made moves to protect the archbishop who was summoned to the place that evening to be warned. Cranmer naively believed that if he were arrested his innocence would protect him but the king was more savvy, knowing that once he was in prison his enemies would make sure that he never came out alive. He gave the archbishop his ring which 'they well know I will use for no other purpose but to call matters from the Council into my own hands to be ordered and determined.'[7]

On the following day Cranmer was accused of 'infecting the whole realm with heresy' as expected, but forewarned Cranmer was able to tell the council that the matter was out of their hands, and he produced the ring to show that the king was serious. Henry then affirmed his full confidence in Cranmer and delivered a not-so-veiled threat to his councillors who sought to overthrow him. Almost immediately those who were calling for his head a few moments before, and certainly included Wriothesley, were anxious to prove that they did not have any dark intentions.

---

7 Nichols, J.G. ed. *Narratives of the Reformation*. (Camden Society, 1859). p 255-8

So why this charade? Henry knew that he had factions within his council and had to contend with them. There is also a suspicion that he was willing to keep his councillors on edge, not knowing which way the wind was blowing. He had agreed to the archbishops arrest the day before and then this elaborate charade had left them all humiliated.

Henry's sixth wife was Catherine Parr, a well-read and intellectually curious woman who was very interested in Protestant reform. The Catholic faction, which included Bishop Gardiner, Lord Rich and Wriothesley, looked upon her suspiciously. They did not approach the queen directly, thinking it more politic to question the ladies of the court to see what they could dig up.

Apparently at this point Wriothesley suggested they bring Anne Askew, a noted Protestant evangeliser, who had been banished to the country in the hope that she would be quiet, back into the frame. She had by this time been examined a second time and sentenced to burning at the stake, but on June 29 she was taken to the Tower to be examined by Wriothesley and Rich. She was questioned for hours but she would not speak thus exasperating her interrogators. Wriothesley summoned the Lieutenant of the Tower, Sir Anthony Knyvet, to prepare the rack.

He did as instructed and she was tied to the rack. Knyvet was not however prepared to do more than "pinch her", in other words give her a light tug to scare her. He would not countenance racking her and ordered his man to set her free. Wriothesley and Rich would have none of it and ordered Knyvet to do as he was told. Knyvet, who may well have ordered and witnessed some brutal treatment of prisoners in the past had his scruples in this instance. It was firstly illegal to rack a woman in Tudor times, moreover it was in the eyes of most people immoral to rack a woman, especially a gentlewoman. He would not budge and was sure that he was in the right.

What happened next was truly astonishing and must forever colour our opinion of Thomas Wriothesley. Seeing that they would not get Knyvet to do or order the work Wriothesley and Rich decided to do the dirty work themselves. They took off their gowns and stepped up to the apparatus to rack this unfortunate woman. Sir Anthony Knyvet, a soldier who had seen more than one battle and probably some of the atrocities of war was appalled and he immediately left the room and the tower wishing to have no part of this act of barbarity.

The two lords continued with their grim work and eventually Anne Askew fainted. She steadfastly refused to incriminate any other person throughout the whole sordid process. Tudor opinion was quite shocked. She had been tried and condemned to the stake, so the law had taken his course and she should have been entitled to have no injury done to her body before the sentence was carried out. The actions of Wriothesly and Rich were against the law, although Wriothesley lamely tried to argue that it was his duty to search out and destroy those who offended against the realm.[8]

It was, in the end, a pointless piece of savagery. Two men, in the highest offices of the land who should have been above such activities demeaned themselves and their cause. One can only assume that Anne Askew's stubbornness drove them beyond reason.

At the time, neither Wriothesley nor Rich suffered. Henry was not particularly interested in the detail of what happened to Anne Askew. She was a heretic. She burned, and that was that. The conservative faction still had their propaganda coup in the burning at the stake and were mostly untroubled by her treatment. Posterity has come to a different judgement and Wriothesley's actions cannot be explained away. It will remain as a permanent stain on a remarkable career.

Undeterred the plotters continued to proceed against the queen thinking that they had the king's approval. She was however warned about what was afoot and she took action herself by speaking directly to Henry and throwing herself on his mercy. She insisted she wold never presume to offer instruction to her king. If she entered into debate with him it was

Queen Anne of Cleves and Queen Catherine Parr

8 Gibbons, Geoffrey. *The Political Career of Thomas Wriothesley, First Earl of Southampton, 1505-1550.* (University of Warwick, 1999). p 80.

only to distract him from his physical pain. She only had his best interests at heart. This (and the story is told by John Foxe) was apparently enough for the king and he was reconciled to her once more.

What followed next was almost comic. Wriothesley had been told by Henry to arrest the Queen in her privy garden one afternoon. Accordingly Wriothesley appeared with a guard of 40 men to arrest her, unaware of the kings change of mind. Instead he met Henry's fiercest hostility rather than acquiescence and he went on his knees to try to plead the agreed arrangements. Henry called him an arrant knave and a fool and asked if they had nothing better to do than try to discover information about a lady who surpassed them all in virtue? "Avaunt my sight!' he thundered and turned his back on Wriothesley, all smiles to the queen.

The persecutions continued for a while but this may have been the peak for the conservatives during Henry's reign. The reformers were soon back in charge of the council and the conservatives would have to wait another six years until Henry's Catholic daughter Mary came to the throne before they could continue their vengeful course. Wriothesley did not live long enough to see the day.

THE DEATH OF A KING

On December 31st 1547 Lord Chancellor Wriothesley, his eyes brimming with tears, announced to Parliament the death of King Henry VIII two days earlier. The sorrow was probably genuine. He had been a dutiful and faithful servant to Henry throughout his reign and it had been the only reign Sir Thomas Wriothesley had known. But there must have been an element of apprehension in his mind. The king he had served so loyally was no longer there to protect him against his enemies, and those enemies were present in the same room.

The main person to watch was Edward Seymour, uncle to the new king. He was Earl of Hertford, shortly to become Duke of Somerset and a protagonist for the evangelical christian faith. Wriothesley was no fool and he had been watching as Seymour had worked to increase his support in Council and push aside the conservative faction. Gardiner, in one of his intemperate moods had got himself banished from court by Henry. The Duke of Norfolk was imprisoned in the tower under sentence of treason and Wriothesley was almost alone to represent the conservative faction and in the meetings that followed he found himself the lone objecting voice. While he was open to reform in his role as a state employee, Wriothesley was a devout Roman Catholic, and the changes under Henry VIII were more a matter of governance than doctrine. The Protestant zeal of Seymour must have created great disquiet in his soul.

Henry VIII in 1542.

On January 31st the executors of Henry's will met to agree on a course of action. They were minded to agree with each other as they knew that they were to be well-rewarded by the terms of Henry's will and nobody was anxious to rock the boat at this early stage. The new council would need an executive head and two new offices were created - Lord Protector of the

Realm and Governor of the King's Person. The executors, and there were sixteen of them, agreed that Edward Seymour should fill both roles with Wriothesley being the lone demurring voice.

Wriothesley, now the earl of Southampton under the terms of Henry's will, began to behave in ways that would have seemed out of character a few days earlier. Whereas he had always been circumspect and careful not to be too far ahead of the pack, he now determined on a course of action he must have known would leave him out in the cold. There was of course no love lost between him and Seymour. They were mutually antipathetic and they had no common ground in their religious beliefs. Nevertheless, Southampton set himself on a course of dissent, believing no doubt that as he was going anyway he might as well go down fighting.

Seymour quickly strengthened his position. The Council of 16 was expanded to 26, all appointed by the Protector. Southampton objected to the legality of this but his objections were ignored. Somerset then accused the Chancellor of legal malpractice. Southampton, in order to make sure he attended all council meetings had offloaded some of his chancery work by delegating the work to other lawyers. This Somerset claimed was illegal and set up a commission to look into the matter. The commission, headed by Sir Richard Rich, upheld the Protector's complaint and Southampton was stripped of the office of Lord Chancellor, confined to his London house and fined the huge sum of £4,000. The restriction to London was designed to keep him from returning to Hampshire and collaborating with Bishop Gardiner, no supporter of the new regime, possibly by raising an army.

Southampton was initially extremely angry at his treatment and to some extent confirmed Somerset's charge that he was unruly and untrustworthy. However he did calm down and return to the level headedness that had served him so well throughout his career. Once he had taken stock of the situation he could see that Seymour would quickly use up any reserves of goodwill. Seymour began to act like Henry VIII but of course he was not Henry. He did not have Henry's political intelligence nor of course did he have the legitimacy of the throne behind him and his increasingly despotic behaviour was bound to alienate his supporters. It was only a matter of time.

The earl of Southampton decided to wait. In the meantime he acted civilly towards Somerset and began to court the friendship of John Dudley, the Earl of Warwick, then the second most powerful man in the kingdom. In a show of humility he offered to exchange houses with Warwick. Ely Place was an appropriate residence for a Lord Chancellor but not for a mere earl so at the end of 1547 Warwick moved into Ely Place and Southampton into Lincoln Place. His good behaviour paid off. His fine was remitted and he was allowed to travel to his estates.

Further political rehabilitation came a year later. Thomas Seymour, the Protector's younger brother embarked on a coup of his own and tried to recruit malcontents to his cause. Southampton was one of them but he was too smart to get embroiled in such a scheme. He reported the interview to the Protector and this act of loyalty got him restored to the Council.

THE FALL

This gave him the opportunity to do the very thing for which he had condemned Thomas Seymour and embark upon a coup of his own. In this case he teamed up with the Earl of Arundel. While Warwick was in eastern England dealing with a revolt and other council members were absent, Southampton and Arundel and their followers seized the Tower. The catholic coup was sudden, unexpected and seemingly complete. Somerset was held a a prisoner.

Warwick returned to London and at a meeting of the whole council a present at Ely Place, Southampton led off by reading the charges against Somerset. Warwick would have none of it. He placed his hand upon his sword and challenged Southampton, "My lord, you seek his blood and he that seeketh his blood would have mine also." This action caused consternation amongst the council and few were ready for a violent confrontation. Most quietly backed away from the Somerset attainder and Southampton found himself stranded and once more out in the cold.

For him it was the end. On January 14th he was dismissed from court and once more place under house arrest. He was now a broken man. For over 20 years he had worked diligently to rise to the very top of the political ladder. He had also made himself a very wealthy man. But now he had burned his bridges and could see no way back. Once again his highly strung temperament induced an illness or weakening of his health. It was believed that he was close to death. Ambassador Van der Velde wrote: "it is supposed that he cannot last two days longer."[9] This was premature. A week later he was showing signs of recovery, but he was not in good spirits. His world had collapsed and there were signs that he had lost the will to live.

Desiring as I am to be under the earth rather than upon it.[10]

He lingered for a few months and on July 30th he died.

Yet he was only 45. He could reasonably expect another 15 years of life and there was nothing in his habits that suggested he was dissolute in his living habits. We do find reports of a periodic fever which would lay him

---

9 *Calendar of State Papers. Spanish* x, 44.
10 Calendar of State Papers. Spanish x 47

Sir Thomas Wriothesley - a drawing by Hans Holbein.

low for a time. One writer has suggested that it was quartan fever and it does appear to have affected him at times of stress. Perhaps he contracted it one more time and at the lowest point in his life he had no strength to fight it.

> My lord Wriothesley, seeing all his heart was opened against him.
> .. And (thinking) this act could never be forgotten, and (because)
> his ambitious mind could take no (lower) place, he killed himself

with sorrow in so much as he said he would not live in such misery"[11]

His only surviving son, Henry, was only five years old. It would be a long wardship until he could achieve hid majority as the 2nd Earl of Southampton. His widow, Jane, was a wealthy woman and was able to secure the charge of her young son and she lived a further 24 years as a dominant figure in her son's life. At his death, the first earl had founded a wealthy family that would continue to have influence for more than another century.

11 Hoak, D.E. *The Kings Council in the Reign of Edward VI.* (Cambridge: Cambridge University Press, 2009). p 257

9 781915 166050